# Poetic Libations

A Poetic Journey Through Tropical Cocktails by

# Diandra Sheppard

Published by

Diandra Sheppard

Atlanta, Georgia

2025

# Poetic Libations

A Poetic Journey Through Tropical Cocktails
**Copyright © 2025 by Diandra Sheppard.**

All rights reserved. No part of this book may be reproduced, distributed, or transmitted in any form or by any means, without the prior written permission of the publisher, except in the case of brief quotations embodied in critical reviews and certain other noncommercial uses permitted by copyright law.

**ISBN: 979-8-9912625-0-7**

**Library of Congress Control Number: 2025907305**

This book is intended for readers of legal drinking age. You must be 21 years or older to legally consume alcoholic beverages in the United States.

Please drink responsibly. Never drink and drive.

Printed in the United States of America

# Prayer to My Highest Power

Please Bless everyone who lays eyes on this prayer.

Console them from the losses they have received.

Enable them to access the excellency within themselves to vibrate loudly.

Dial up their discernment so they navigate this realm aware. Hold their hands and lead them to trees that bear fruits.

Function as a microphone for those whose voices need help being heard.

Wipe the dust from their eyes to help them see clarity.

May their ancestors hold their hands and lead them to the light when they are surrounded by darkness.

Mold their mindsets.

Manifest their destinies by the power of their tongues.

May they succeed without fear.

Assist them in areas they are lacking.

Make them use your words to keep warm from the coldness of the world.

Pour out your blessings on them.

Protect them from the zombies of this world. Bring ambition out of the confused and boldness out of the weak.

Give them the fortitude to withstand storms with poise calmness to a future where they will be joyful and unrestrained.

Although life can be hard, forbid us to quit on ourselves.

Amen.

# Tables of Contents

Introduction ................................................................. ix
Peeling Back Layers ...................................................... 1
Soursop Lemon Pop ..................................................... 3
Guyanese Atlien ............................................................ 5
Sweetest Thing ............................................................. 8
What A Charmer ......................................................... 10
Coco Loco .................................................................... 12
The Hero Within Me ................................................... 14
Stush Like My Liquor .................................................. 16
Intensity ...................................................................... 18
Bronzed By Hennessy ................................................. 20
A Poem For My Mom ................................................. 22
Sangria Sunrise ........................................................... 23
Lions Don't Born Sheep .............................................. 26
Smoking Sorrel ........................................................... 28
Hypnosis ..................................................................... 31
100Degrees ................................................................. 33
GT Sugar ...................................................................... 36
Pattycake Pink ............................................................ 38
Woman of My Dreams ............................................... 40
Brunch Rum Punch .................................................... 42
    Synchronicities ..................................................... 52

Metamorphosis..................................................................57

Marked With The Greats ...........................................61

I'm So ATL...................................................................65

Athenas Battle Cry ....................................................69

Closing........................................................................71

Diandra's Bar Gospel......................................................78

About the Author............................................................83

**A Tiny Whisper Before We Start…**

Go to Diandra's Bar Gospel in the back if you want to pour what you feel and sip what you dream—if your lips yearn for something more than words.

The instruments, the spirits, and the mysteries are all there.

A sensual cheat sheet for crafting cocktails that kiss back.

Take a deep drink. Slowly stir.

Allow pleasure to direct the pour.

# Introduction

How haunting and eerie the mind wanders when confronted with a harsh reality. In difficult times, I turn to my creator. On one such an occasion, I closed my eyes, prayed, and received a vision: It was me publishing a book featuring my cocktails and poetry. I've worked as a bartender in Atlanta for many years both in craft bars and clubs, where quality and presentation are everything. This book is a reflection of my deep passion for both mixology and poetry. It's not just a traditional cocktail recipe book it's a tribute to the art of cocktails. Many of my creations have been tested and celebrated at the events I've worked, proving their worth time and again. Whether you're hosting an event or planning a romantic date night, these recipes will elevate the experience. With this book in hand, you won't need to search far for exceptional cocktails.

**Sincerely,**

**A Mahogany Divinity in the Flesh!**

## Peeling Back Layers

I've poured my heart out for all to see, unveiling the deeper layers of me. I've tapped into energies rich and true, infused with cultural specialties too. Now, enjoy my poetic pleasantries.

# Soursop Lemon Pop

**Ingredients:**

1.5 oz gin

0.5 oz Huana Mayan Guanabana Rum Liqueur

0.5 lemon

0.5 oz champagne

Lemon twist for garnish (optional)

**Instructions:**

Fill a cocktail shaker with ice.

Add 1.5 oz of gin to the shaker.

Pour in 0.5 oz of Huana Mayan Guanabana Rum Liqueur.

Add 0.5 oz of lemon to the shaker.

For 15 seconds, give the mixture a vigorous shake to mix the flavors and chill the beverage.

The cocktail should be strained into a chilled highball glass.

Top it off with 0.5 oz of champagne or sparkling white wine.

For an added touch of presentation, rim the glass with sugar or garnish the drink with a twist of lemon.

Serve and enjoy your Soursop Lemon Pop cocktail!

## **Guyanese Atlien**

Been around the world, all across the seas

A military brat, but Atlanta adopted me   It's not like

Miami. We don't kick it on a beach   We party in

our shades, clubbing after 3

Covington Highway for chow mein and chicken curry

But I'll take a 10-piece and fries. Don't forget my sweet tea

I hustled in 4th ward; it woke up the Komodo dragon in me

Chuck up the deuce or the 4, Hell maybe the E

My tower card happened to me when I was in the AUC

Took it to the chin so hard I got knocked to my knees

Times were hard, but I prevailed. Just had to find my steez

Ate food off China, sipped African teas

Still got it out of the mud; call me Chameleon Dee

I feel like Lauryn Hill life is the sweetest thing

Shout out Champagne Trap, P99 to infinity

Walk it like I talk it, the Atlanta recipe

Confident, and I know it, you should want a woman like me

Blazing hot from Mars, with a star girl destiny.

# Sweetest Thing

**Ingredients:**

2 oz Patrón Silver Tequila

1 oz lychee syrup

0.5 oz pineapple juice

0.5 oz fresh lemon juice

Lychee fruit or a sugar rim for garnish (optional)

**Instructions:**

Place a martini glass in the freezer for 10–15 minutes to chill.

Fill a cocktail shaker with ice to ensure a cold, refreshing mix.

Add 2 oz of Patrón Silver Tequila.

Pour in 0.5 oz of pineapple juice and 1 oz of lychee syrup.

Squeeze in 0.5 oz of fresh lemon juice to balance the sweetness with a tart twist.

Secure the shaker and shake vigorously for 15–20 seconds until well-chilled.

Strain into the chilled martini glass, using a finemesh strainer if needed to remove ice shards or pulp.

Garnish with a lychee fruit or a twist of lemon for a sophisticated finish.

Serve and enjoy your Sweetest Thing Martini!

## **What A Charmer**

Ever since I could remember, I've been poppin' my collar

Men now call me cocky because they failed at their

holler

Don't be mad at me, sir. Blame it on my father! Majestic like my mama might twirl a wand like Harry Potter

Why try to humble women who are sexy and even smarter?

Could lick you like a sucker, but I instead move with honor

My smile may make you lucid, but remember, I'm a charmer

Sweet like Cocoa and I'm Loco, did you forget to peep the collar?

# Coco Loco

**Ingredients:**

2 oz tequila (preferably silver or blanco for a clean, crisp flavor)

1 oz coconut syrup (for a rich, tropical taste)

1 oz fresh lime juice

½ oz simple syrup (adjust to taste)

Lime wheel and mint sprig for garnish (optional)

**Instructions:**

Fill a cocktail shaker with ice.

Add 2 oz of tequila.

Pour in 1 oz of coconut cream for a smooth, tropical richness.

Squeeze in 1 oz of fresh lime juice for a bright citrusy balance.

Add ½ oz of simple syrup, adjusting based on the sweetness of your coconut cream.

Shake vigorously for 15–20 seconds to blend the flavors and chill the drink.

Strain into a glass and garnish with a lime wheel and mint sprig for a refreshing touch.

Serve and enjoy your Coco Loco!

## **The Hero Within Me**

I will allow myself to save myself   I am my hero

Adorning myself in armor, refusing to falter

I will not be the damsel in distress

I am the Dame

I can make men kneel and kiss my feet

I am Her! The One, never secondary

The blooming rosebush in the garden

I am a sight to see

The evolution I seek is within me

Stush like my liquor, lifting minds like speed.

I'm here for a reason: the universe acknowledges me Making you fall in love as if I were Aphrodite.

# **Stush Like My Liquor**

1 oz whiskey

0.5 oz fresh tangerine juice

1 oz brut Champagne or sparkling wine

2 dashes orange bitters

tangerine or orange peel (for garnish)

**Instructions:**

Fill a cocktail shaker with ice.

Add 1 oz of whiskey.

Pour in 0.5 oz of fresh tangerine juice.

Add 2 dashes of orange bitters.

Shake vigorously for 15 seconds to blend the flavors and chill the drink.

Strain into a chilled champagne flute.

Top with 1 oz of Brut Champagne or sparkling wine.

Gently stir to incorporate the ingredients.

Garnish with a twist of tangerine or orange peel for an elegant finish.

Serve and enjoy your Stush Like My Liquor!

## __Intensity__

Must I forget my ancestors' pedigree   Simply because I adapt effortlessly?

Sweet and bronzed like Hennessy,

Yet GT blood still runs through me.

They didn't leave their guava trees  For

me to erase their legacy!

Their presence lingers heavily

Me, plus he, plus all of thee

The magnitude of our existence is an entity

Can't you feel it

The intensity?

# Bronzed By Hennessy

**Ingredients:**

1.5 oz Hennessy Cognac

0.5 oz peach schnapps

0.5 oz orange juice

0.5 oz cranberry juice

0.5 oz strawberry purée

0.5 oz fresh lemon juice

Orange slice or strawberry (for garnish, optional)

**Instructions:**

Fill a cocktail shaker with ice.

Add 1.5 oz of Hennessy Cognac.

Pour in 0.5 oz of peach schnapps.

Add 0.5 oz each of orange juice and cranberry juice.

Mix in 0.5 oz of strawberry purée.

Squeeze in 0.5 oz of fresh lemon juice.

Shake vigorously for 15 seconds to blend flavors and chill the drink.

Strain into an ice-filled highball glass.

Garnish with a strawberry or an orange slice for an elegant touch.

Serve and enjoy your Bronzed by Hennessy!

## **A Poem For My Mom**

Goddess of the hunt,

Goddess of the moon,

Your smile glows like a Sangria Sunrise in June

May you drum to your own beat, dance to your tune,

Ground yourself in your garden watch your flowers bloom

Never walk this Earth with your head bowed in gloom,

You're a champion by birth, from your great granny's womb.

A warrior on Earth, victorious in every room,

Romantic by nature love is your perfume

Your creativity is galactic, like Pharaohs in their tombs,

Queen of the pack, leader of the platoon

Ground yourself in your garden watch the world bloom!

## **Sangria Sunrise**

**Ingredients:**

1.5 oz tequila

3 oz red wine (a fruity red like Spanish Tempranillo works best)

2 oz orange juice

0.5 oz raspberry syrup

Orange slice and maraschino cherry (for garnish)

**Instructions:**

Fill a highball or wine glass with ice.

Pour 1.5 oz of tequila over the ice.

Carefully layer 3 oz of red wine on top of the tequila.

Slowly pour 2 oz of orange juice over the back of a spoon to create a layered effect.

Drizzle 0.5 oz of raspberry syrup down the side of the glass to achieve the signature sunrise look.

Garnish with an orange slice and a maraschino cherry.

Give it a gentle stir before sipping to blend the flavors.

Serve and enjoy your Sangria Sunrise!

## **Lions Don't Born Sheep**

Do you hear my roar?

Do you see my stride?

I am Shep's daughter, and I yell it with pride

From the top of the hill to the bottom of the slide

He wiped my tears when I stumbled and cried,

When I wandered and got lost, he was my guide.

An army veteran ranger, a true winner by my side

I stepped into the jungle, feeling shy,

But wisdom from the Lion taught me to rise

There's no such thing as luck it's all about time

Luck is just preparation meeting opportunity so shine

I'm locked in, focused, my eye on the prize

Smoking hot with Sorrel what a pleasant surprise

Now it's time to announce the Queen has arrived!

# Smoking Sorrel

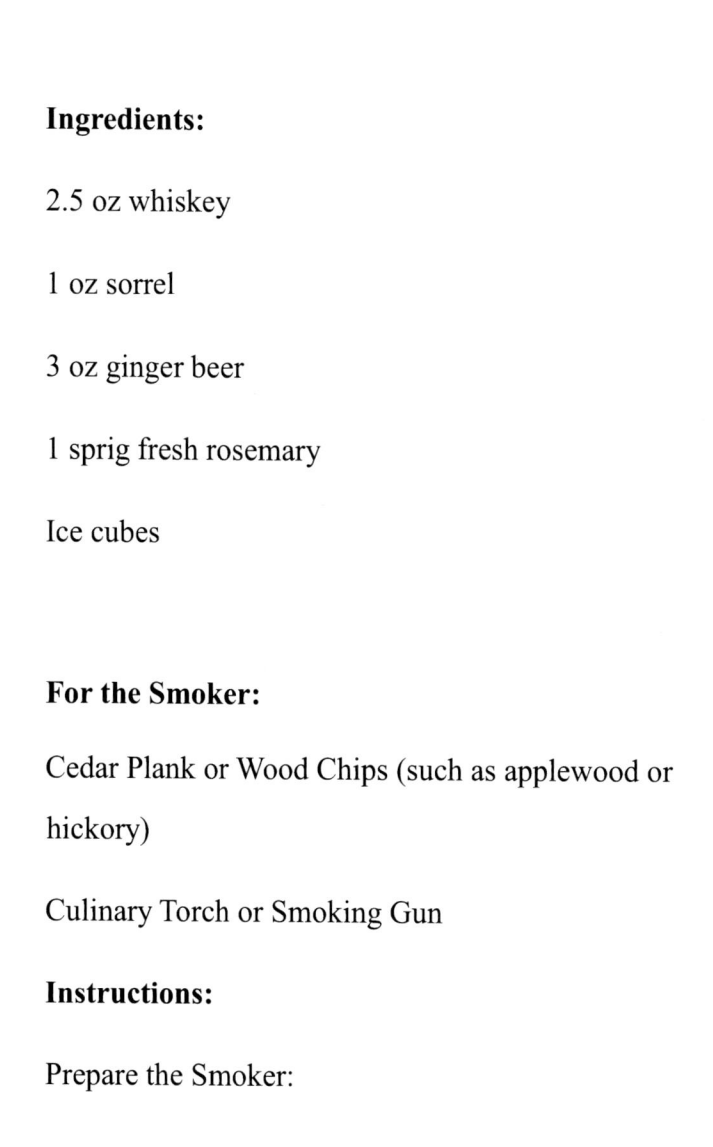

**Ingredients:**

2.5 oz whiskey

1 oz sorrel

3 oz ginger beer

1 sprig fresh rosemary

Ice cubes

**For the Smoker:**

Cedar Plank or Wood Chips (such as applewood or hickory)

Culinary Torch or Smoking Gun

**Instructions:**

Prepare the Smoker:

Place the cedar plank or wood chips on a heat-safe surface.

Using a culinary torch or smoking gun, ignite the wood until it begins to produce smoke.

Cover the plank or chips with a glass or shaker tin to trap the smoke.

**Prepare the Cocktail:**

In a mixing glass or cocktail shaker, combine 2.5 oz whiskey and 1 oz sorrel. Stir well to blend.

Take the overturned glass from the smoking setup and pour in the whiskey and sorrel mixture. Let it sit for about 10 seconds to infuse the smoky flavor.

Fill a mule mug (or preferred serving glass) with ice cubes.

Strain the smoked whiskey and sorrel mixture into the mug.

Top with 3 oz ginger beer, leaving space for garnish.

Garnish with a sprig of fresh rosemary for an aromatic touch.

Serve and enjoy your Smoking Sorrel!

## **Hypnosis**

Prepare to be hypnotized

By the magic of this fruit

A natural sweetness on your tongue, No flavor more astute. Eyes grow wide, smiles shine bright, With just a single bite. So pleasurable, so decadent A truly splendid delight!

# 100Degrees

**Ingredients:**

1.5 oz tequila

2 oz pineapple juice

1–2 slices Jalapeño (adjust to your spice preference)

1 oz triple sec (or orange liqueur)

1 oz fresh lemon juice

**Instructions:**

Prepare your glass: Use a rocks glass or margarita glass. If you prefer extra heat, muddle one jalapeño slice at the bottom.

Fill the glass with ice to chill the cocktail and slightly dilute the flavors.

**In a cocktail shaker, combine:**

1.5 oz tequila

2 oz pineapple juice

1 oz triple sec

1 oz fresh lemon juice

Another jalapeño slice (if you want it spicier).

Shake vigorously for 15–20 seconds to blend and chill the ingredients.

Strain the cocktail into your prepared glass over the ice.

Optionally, garnish with a jalapeño slice or pineapple wedge for a finishing touch.

Gently stir to evenly distribute the spice, if desired.

Enjoy your 100Degrees Margarita responsibly!

**Pro Tips:**

Adjust the amount of jalapeño to your spice level.

Prefer it sweeter? Add a touch of simple syrup to balance the flavors!

## **GT Sugar**

Brown like sugar, I'm too sweet to beat

Initiation begins; now it's time to compete I choose only winners losers bow in defeat,

Mending broken hearts, making them complete

My road leads to Heaven, no two-way street   Stay

out of my oven if you can't take the heat

Fire fuels my desire, so my pattycake stays pink

Thoughts so magnetic, you echo what I think

# Pattycake Pink

**Ingredients:**

1 oz Piñaq Liqueur

1.5 oz Grey Goose Vodka (or your preferred vodka)

0.5 oz cranberry juice

0.5 oz lingonberry syrup

0.5 oz fresh lime juice

Lime twist or cranberry (for garnish)

**Instructions:**

Fill a cocktail shaker with ice.

Add 1 oz of Piñaq Liqueur.

Pour in 1.5 oz of Grey Goose Vodka.

Add 0.5 oz each of cranberry juice and lingonberry syrup.

Squeeze in 0.5 oz of fresh lime juice.

Shake vigorously for 15 seconds to mix and chill the flavors.

Strain into a chilled martini glass.

Garnish with a lime twist or cranberry for an elegant touch.

Serve and enjoy your Pattycake Pink!

## **Woman of My Dreams**

I woke up as the woman of my dreams

God knows the time it took to be

When life reminded me of humility,

I pressed my lips closed and let my actions speak

It allowed my love to flow, pure and clean

It's not my issue if others misread me

All I've done is ignite the spark within

Even when slung in mud, I moved like a deity

Battle wounds add character,

Like a movie star on screen.

Ran over hurdles, let my mind roam free

Brunch rum punches I savor, especially overseas

Dropped my pride, removed my ego

Now my heart is filled with glee.

# **Brunch Rum Punch**

**Ingredients:**

2 oz dark rum

1 oz pineapple juice

1 oz cranberry juice

1 oz orange juice

0.5 oz fresh lime juice

2 dashes Angostura Bitters

Brut Champagne or Sparkling Wine (to top)

**Instructions:**

Fill a cocktail shaker with ice.

Add 2 oz of Dark Rum.

Pour in 1 oz each of pineapple juice, cranberry juice, and orange juice.

Squeeze in 0.5 oz of fresh lime juice.

Add 2 dashes of Angostura Bitters.

Shake vigorously for 15 seconds to blend flavors and chill the drink.

Fill a highball glass with ice.

Strain the cocktail over the ice.

Top with Brut Champagne or sparkling wine for a bubbly finish.

Serve and enjoy your refreshing Brunch Rum Punch!

The Empress with her cocktail

A hot tub and cold drinks

*Cups up*

*Looking smooth drinking even smoother*

## The Art Of Kintsugi

Once the anger passed, now my eyes were all swollen.

I had to read the room before I chose to be outspoken.

I had to swallow pride to stop my heart from being frozen.

I had to change my ways—like Romans in the slogan.

I had to be the general, like the Japanese Shogun.

I was initially disillusioned, but my mind is now open.

I had a birth chart reading—I had zero degrees.

Then he posed the question: —What type of king will you be?

Will you help your people, or sit in your castle and feast?|

I said I wanna pop rubber bands and be like T.I.P.

I wanna be good in every zone and bust my shoulder lean.

I wanna be Gucci in the streets where I reside and rule the East.

I wanna enjoy the French 75s and see the world with ease.

I wanna sip my cocktails and dress fly to match the breeze.

I wanna be pretty with intellect—like the breed Siamese.

I wanna be so kind, they use their free will for me.

I had to break my mind and fuse it—just like Kintsugi,

In the South of America, where the golds are

Guyanese

*Cheers to trips across the seas*

## Synchronicities

I had to book a trip, across

the great big seas.


I arrived happily, but

got called instantly.


I answered… and

walked to the ocean.

The water looked so clean.


I crawled and hesitated — now

I'm seeing things.

Wiped my eyes…

and saw a reflection, smiling,

blowing kisses at me.

Am I hallucinating?

Or are these spirits communicating?

I put my hands in the water — they

tried to take my rings.

I stepped back in denial.

Man… this couldn't be. Got

possessed by a power…

maybe it's rum from Belize.

These aren't even my ancestors — what would they want from me? I leaned forward to take a closer look... and it was my face, gleaming.

I whispered to the spirit:

—Are you you, or are you me?

No response was heard, but I could feel the instant breeze.

Did I live here in a past life?

Is this why I'm on my knees? I heard a voice in my spirit —

sharp enough to make me freeze:

**"Your chapter has begun.**

**The power of knowledge comes with keys.**

You've bartered with your life — don't get full off bread and cheese.

Don't upset yourself with disappointment; the losses are just a tease. When life gave you lemons, you juiced them creatively.

Life's a roller coaster… filled with synchronicities."

I opened my eyes, full of tears — sixth

sense abilities.

I guess it is time to fulfill my purpose… escape

this enmity.

Hennessy Bronzed

## Metamorphosis

Once I opened the door to impending doom,

I closed my eyes and let my dreams be the

path out of the room.

I was so hurt,

I could fume!

Had to get up on my Zoom,

and be more strategic with

the lies that I consume.

Might just pop it like a balloon — but

don't treat me like a buffoon.

I was stuck in the web,

like a caterpillar in a cocoon.

I had to isolate my fire, like

lava in a lagoon.

Poured my drinks so strong, you'd

think they came from the moon.

Pomegranate liqueur makes

it the color of maroon.

I even learned to change my tune, like

I owned a bassoon.

On my Warren G tip — so

explosive, I might boom.


I just prayed for sunnier days…

I hated shining in the gloom.


But like a rose, I bloomed — after

death, life resumed.


Now I sip with purpose — strategic

with the cocktails I choose

Player 99 until infinity

## Marked With The Greats

I don't have much time to give —

I'm tryna make it shake, with

rings all over my fingers like it's

1988.

I'll be fly and off the chain until

I see those pearly gates. I've

been showing only love —

I'm confused by all the hate.

Told my family I love them,

and in the end, it'll be straight.

Loyalty and authenticity might

be my favorite traits.

Put shades on my third eye — silly geese took the

bait. Taurus moon, so I'm like Whitaker in the film

where he debates.

My waist looks good — it eights,

tequila shots across the states.

Historic times we're living in — so

mark me with the greats.

Rub me wrong and I might grate,

send you packing like you're freight.

Too Atlanta with my game — like

I'm in Cascade with the skates.

Smooth like Hennessy, and

I'm sweet like it — don't

talk money, can't translate.


I'm on fire right now presently— does

it look like I can wait?

Does it look like I'll be late?

Don't come near me if you lack faith.


I had to chuckle at that prior line —

kinda fear that I might ate. Causing

hell like the angel Lucifer, with

those sixes on my plates

*Testing recipes while turning heads*

## I'm So ATL

I'm so futuristic, looking like Young

Dro in my Polo — New Edition, keep

it a tradition.

I'm so ATL, gotta speak it

with conviction. I'm so ATL,

I stay away from politicians

and the politicking' — that's

a contradiction.

I'm so ATL, addictions conquer

the opposition.

I'm so ATL,

they're in a strip club with prescriptions.

I'm so ATL,

I execute with precision.

Sip martinis in bikinis —

a bad chick militia, a bad

bitch conscription.

Rich Kidz, my patna dem —

Will be sung like an inscription.

Could never be R. Kelly, but

the keys in the ignition.

The land of sedition — I'm so ATL, how could I ask for permission?

I'm so ATL, we don't need an intermission. I'm so ATL, you better watch your diction.

*The Sea of Dee*

## Athenas Battle Cry

I know my shell is so pretty, but I come from Mars

Ares in the stars, that's why I'm riddled with these scars.

I can't turn the cheek, smoke opposition in cigars.

Something about their cries reminds me of Santana with guitars.

I know my power, I could write your name and freeze it in a jar.

Athena in the stars, you better run from me and go far.

Let me catch you i'd shred you, cook you until you charr.

Hand out your limbs to my dogs, love to see them snarl.

Hate me like I'm Chris, put money on the floor, and see my gnarly.

Take food from my mouth, I'd bite your hand like I'm Charlie.

Ops she bit my finger, now the poison lingers.

Cripple your body, I'm a hybrid of venom and whiskers.

I'm a thinker and I see your ego and triggers.

I can steal your lover all it takes is an eye and some whispers.

Make you a pawn in my game, spend your check on some strippers.

What can I say, I'm from Atlanta and I love the tippers.

Think I'm green and I'll cut your flippers with these scissors.

I'm so hot right now, I can whip you in a drink with mixers.

Does that mean I'm bitter? That's what the world would say.

I'm an army brat things have to go my way.

I know the answers, hear me ye?

Baby I'm not sway, small in size but a don dada in my weight.

## Closing

I've poured my spirit for all to taste,

no drop of truth has gone to waste.

Each word, each mix, a legacy — a

toast to love, and ancestry.

The garnish, the sugar rim, and the main pour

*I pour with passion, they enjoy in lust*

Gathering of Goddesses and

We poured like poetry

Champagne Trap for Mayor

*High in spirits pouring spirits*

When the waters blue we drink 1942

# Diandra's Bar Gospel

## A Sultry Scripture For The Sacred Art Of Sipping.

## Bar Confessions

| Tool | Purpose |
| --- | --- |
| Shaker | For mixing cocktails |
| Jigger | For accurate mixer and spirit measures |
| Bar Spoon | Perfect for mixing or arranging materials in layers |
| Muddler | For added flavor, crush fresh fruit, herbs, or sugar |
| Strainer | Keeps sediments and ice out of your last pour |
| Juicer | For fresh citrus to add color to beverages |
| Peeler | Use ornamental twists or citrus peels as garnish |

| | |
|---|---|
| Torch | Caramelize sweets, flame garnishes, or add smokey flair |
| Mesh Sieve | For delicate cocktails that require double straining |
| Mule Mug | Serving cold tropical cocktails in a traditional copper vessel |

When possible, use top shelf; your cocktail is worthy of a high-end pen.

Prices may differ slightly depending on the area.

# Spirited Affairs

| Spirit Category | Premium Brands | Premium Price (ATL) | BudgetFriendly Sub's | Budget Price (ATL) | Notes |
|---|---|---|---|---|---|
| Vodka | Tito's, Belvedere, Ketel One | $22–$32 | Svedka, New Amsterdam, Deep Eddy | $10–$15 | Perfect for fruitbased cocktails, it is smooth and mixable. |
| Rum | Wray & Nephew, El Dorado, Diplomatico | $25–$35 | Cruzan, Bacardi 4 Year, Don Q | $12–$18 | Light, adaptable, and having an island feel. |
| Tequila | Casamigos, Fortaleza, Espolon | $28–$45 | Lunazul, Cimarron, El Jimador | $18–$22 | Excellent for smoky or citrusforward cocktails. |
| Gin | Hendrick's, Tanqueray Ten, Botanist | $30–$42 | Seagram's Extra Dry, New Amsterdam | $11–$15 | Works great with flower blends or spritzes. |

| | | | | | |
|---|---|---|---|---|---|
| Whiskey/ Bourbon | Uncle Nearest, Woodford Reserve, Crown Royal | $28–$38 | Evan Williams Black, Old Forester | $13–$18 | Smooth enough for sipping, strong for mixing. |
| Liqueurs | Piñaq, Grand Marnier, Huana Mayan Guanabana | $18–$24 | Rumchata, Cointreau, E&J Peach | $11–$16 | Save money on brand names while keeping flavor tropical. |
| Sweet Wine | Spanish Tempranillo | $10–$15 | Yellow Tail Sweet Red, Carlo Rossi Sangria | $6–$10 | Good for sangrias and winebased cocktails. |

**Pro Tip:** Use fresh ingredients and high-quality spirits in combination; flavor should always entice rather than compete

**Cocktail Cost & Remix**

Each cocktail recipe is based on two-ounce pours, with every standard bottle yielding roughly 12–13 drinks.

**Temptation tactics**

For those who like their kisses less sugary:

A splash of club soda can work wonders.

Let the bubbles balance your bowl—

Tame the sweet, save the soul.

These recipes are your foundation, but

you are always free to remix each sip.

## About the Author

Diandra Sheppard is a poet of pleasure and memory, a curator of cocktails steeped in soul and story. Born in Memphis and shaped by the nomadic rhythm of military life, she carries with her the flavors of many places and the pulse of a rich Guyanese heritage. Now rooted in Atlanta, she finds inspiration in the city's sultry nights, vibrant gatherings, and the quiet poetry of a well-poured drink. Poetic Libations: A Poetic Journey Through Tropical Cocktails is her love letter to ritual and revelry—a collection that stirs the senses and toasts to culture, connection, and slow-burning joy.

**Follow her journey on Instagram:**
**@deewiththelionheart**

Made in the USA
Columbia, SC
07 August 2025